The Cherokee
and Their History

by Mary Englar

Content Adviser: Bruce Bernstein, Ph.D.,
Assistant Director for Cultural Resources
National Museum of the American Indian, Smithsonian Institution

Reading Adviser: Rosemary G. Palmer, Ph.D.,
Department of Literacy, College of Education,
Boise State University

COMPASS POINT BOOKS
MINNEAPOLIS, MINNESOTA

Compass Point Books
3109 West 50th Street, #115
Minneapolis, MN 55410

Visit Compass Point Books on the Internet at *www.compasspointbooks.com*
or e-mail your request to *custserv@compasspointbooks.com*

On the cover: Cherokee trading party, ca. 1762

Photographs ©: Courtesy Frank H. McClung Museum, The University of Tennessee, Knoxville, painting by Greg Harlin, cover, 19; Prints Old & Rare, back cover (far left); Library of Congress, back cover, 4, 5, 12, 33, 34, 35, 36, 37; Woolaroc Museum, Bartlesville, Oklahoma, 7; Marc Muench/Corbis, 9; The Granger Collection, New York, 11, 29, 32; Kit Breen, 14, 15, 20; Cherokee Historical Association, 17; North Wind Picture Archives, 18; Dorothy Tidwell Sullivan, 21, 22, 25; Richard A. Cooke/Corbis, 23; James P. Rowan, 24; Art Resource, N.Y., 26; MPI/Getty Images, 27, 31; Talmadge Davis, 30; Peter Turnley/Corbis, 38; Courtesy The Echota Cherokee Tribe of Alabama/photo by Nathanael Richardson, 40; AP Photo/Tulsa World/A. Cuervo, 41.

Editor: Julie Gassman
Designer/Page Production: Bradfordesign, Inc./Bobbie Nuytten
Photo Researcher: Svetlana Zhurkin
Cartographer: XNR Productions, Inc.
Educational Consultant: Diane Smolinski
Library Consultant: Kathleen Baxter

Managing Editor: Catherine Neitge
Creative Director: Keith Griffin
Editorial Director: Carol Jones

Library of Congress Cataloging-in-Publication Data
Englar, Mary.
  The Cherokee and their history / by Mary Englar.
      p. cm—(We the people)
  Includes bibliographical references and index.
  ISBN-13: 978-0-7565-1273-6 (hardcover)
  ISBN-10: 0-7565-1273-5 (hardcover)
  ISBN-13: 978-0-7565-2497-5 (paperback)
  ISBN-10: 0-7565-2497-0 (paperback)
  1. Cherokee Indians—History—Juvenile literature. 2. Cherokee Indians—Social life and customs—Juvenile literature. I. Title. II. We the people (Series) (Compass Point Books)
  E99.C5S67 2006
  975.004'97557—dc22   2005003677

 This book was manufactured with paper containing at least 10 percent post-consumer waste.

TABLE OF CONTENTS

The Trail Where They Cried 4

Who Are the Cherokee? 9

Life in the Appalachians 14

Town Living 19

In Balance with Nature 25

"We Have Now Given the White Men
Enough Land" 27

"Our Country and Our People" 33

The Cherokee Today 38

Glossary 42

Did You Know? 43

Important Dates 44

Important People 45

Want to Know More? 46

Index 48

THE TRAIL WHERE THEY CRIED

The Cherokee Indians were about to face much suffering in the days ahead. It was the spring of 1838, and 7,000 U.S. soldiers, led by U.S. Major General Winfield Scott, had arrived in Cherokee land to round up the 15,000 Cherokee Indians. The U.S. government was forcing the Cherokee to leave their homeland in the Appalachian Mountains. Soon they would have to travel hundreds of miles to Indian Territory in what is now known as Oklahoma. The Cherokee knew that the move was coming,

Winfield Scott

but they hoped their chief, John Ross, could convince the government to let them stay on their farms.

While Chief Ross was in Washington, D.C., the roundup at home moved quickly. Families were taken from their homes and fields and put into stockades. The Cherokee were forced to stay in prison for months and

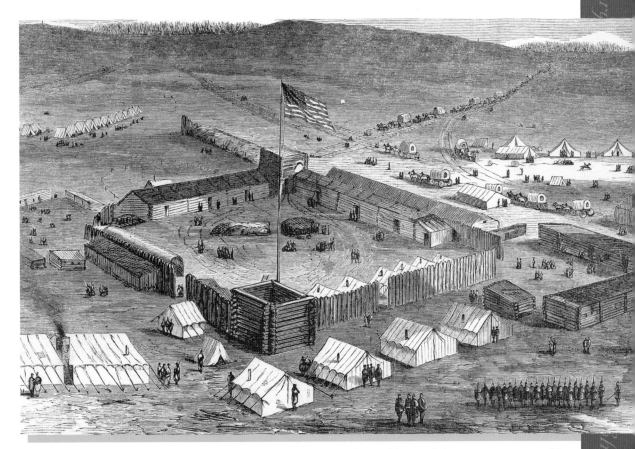

This illustration of a military stockade appeared in Harper's Weekly *in 1869.*

wait for transportation to the West. Many were not allowed to pack clothing, bedding, or food. Their living quarters were cramped and dirty. Soon the old and very young Cherokee began to get sick from disease and die.

Chief Ross returned home in July 1838 and saw the misery of his people. He had not convinced the government to change its plan. So Chief Ross began to plan for the journey. He divided his people into groups of 1,000. Each group received wagons, supplies, and horses. The wagons carried the sick and the supplies, but most Cherokee had to walk.

The groups began to leave the stockades in September. They were given enough food for 80 days. One soldier wrote, "I saw the helpless Cherokee arrested and dragged from their homes. … And in the chill of a drizzling rain on an October morning I saw them loaded like cattle or sheep into 645 wagons."

A few days after the first group left, another followed. Soon, thousands of Cherokee followed a trail that led across

Tennessee, Kentucky, Missouri, and Arkansas. They walked for nearly 800 miles (1,280 kilometers). When the groups became sick, they traveled only a few miles each day. It took some groups six months to reach Indian Territory.

Winter came early that year. Without blankets, warm clothing, or food, many people got sick. They died

The Trail of Tears, *a well-recognized painting by Robert Lindneux, hangs in Woolaroc Museum in Bartlesville, Oklahoma.*

7

from hunger, cold, and disease. The Cherokee buried many people along the trail. Chief Ross lost his wife to pneumonia.

The Cherokee remember this terrible journey as the Trail Where They Cried. One elder later recalled, "Long time we travel on way to new land. People feel bad when they leave Old Nation. Women cry and made sad wails. Children cry and many men cry, and all look sad like when friends die."

By the time the last group of Cherokee arrived in Oklahoma, more than 4,000 people had died. Today, this journey is remembered as the Trail of Tears. Most Cherokee never returned to their homelands in the Appalachian Mountains.

WHO ARE THE CHEROKEE?

The ancestors of the Cherokee lived in the valleys of the southern Appalachian Mountains for hundreds of years before Europeans came to North America. Historians are not sure when they came to these mountains, but some believe they traveled south from the Great Lakes.

The Cherokee's forested homeland was filled with a great variety of foods. Deer provided food, clothing, and tools. Bears provided warm robes and cooking grease. The Cherokee people built

Cherokee National Forest lies in the southern Appalachian Mountains in Tennessee.

9

their towns on good farmland along streams and lakes. Women planted gardens with corn, beans, pumpkins, and sunflowers. They also harvested many kinds of wild vegetables, fruits, and nuts.

The Cherokee's name came from a neighboring tribe. The Creek Indians called them chilokee, which means "people of a different speech." The Cherokee called themselves Ani-Yunwiya, which means the "real people."

At the end of the 1600s, European traders came to the Cherokee homelands. The Cherokee traded deerskins and animal furs for the Europeans' guns, metal pots, and cloth. During times of war and American growth in the 1700s, the Cherokee lost much of their land, and they adopted many of their American neighbors' ways. They still lived in towns, but many also lived on large farms where they raised cattle and crops. Most wore American clothing and lived in houses and log cabins.

In 1830, the U.S. government passed the Indian Removal Act. This law forced all American Indians in the

Indians traded furs for European goods.

eastern United States to move from their homelands to
Indian Territory in the West. The Cherokee did not want
to leave, and they fought the new law in court. Although
the U.S. Supreme Court ruled in 1832 that the Cherokee

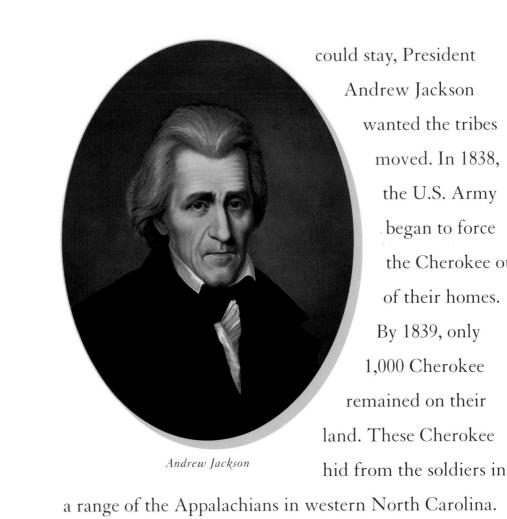

Andrew Jackson

could stay, President Andrew Jackson wanted the tribes moved. In 1838, the U.S. Army began to force the Cherokee out of their homes. By 1839, only 1,000 Cherokee remained on their land. These Cherokee hid from the soldiers in a range of the Appalachians in western North Carolina.

Today, more than 281,000 Cherokee live in the United States. The majority live in Oklahoma, but more than 8,000 still live in North Carolina. They make up one of the largest tribes in the United States. About half of the Cherokee live on reservations, but others live in every state

in the United States. In the last 30 years, the Cherokee
Nation of Oklahoma has built schools and health clinics
and created jobs for the Cherokee people.

The Cherokee took four different routes on their Trail of Tears journey.

13

LIFE IN THE APPALACHIANS

The Cherokee lived in towns in the highlands and river valleys of the southern Appalachian Mountains. Great forests of oak, pine, maple, and chestnut trees covered the land. The Cherokee made clearings for their towns by cutting down trees and burning the brush. Most towns had between 30 and 60 houses.

Families worked together to build and repair their houses. First, they cut straight trees to use for the corner

14

Small mud and clay houses with solid roofs served as winter homes for the Cherokee.

In addition to community crops, each family grew their own small garden.

posts. For the walls, they tied woven branches to the
frame. They plastered the branches inside and out with
a mixture of mud and grass. Roofs were covered with tree
bark or grass. They left a hole in the roof to let the smoke
escape from their cooking fire.

The community worked together in the spring to
plant corn, beans, squash, and sunflowers. Corn was the
most important crop because it provided large stores of
food for the Cherokee. After a summer of growth, the
townspeople let the corn and beans dry in the fields.

Then, they worked together to bring in the harvest. The women spent many hours grinding the dried corn into meal to make bread. Sometimes they added nuts or beans to the bread mixture.

Cherokee women owned the houses, the household goods, and the town gardens they planted. Women and girls spent much of their time tending the fields. They also gathered wild vegetables and roots in the nearby forests and swamps. Summers brought ripe blueberries, mulberries, raspberries, and grapes. In the fall, they collected acorns, walnuts, hickory nuts, and chestnuts. Mothers taught their daughters to leave several of the first plants they saw, to show nature they were not greedy. When they picked wild plants, they left behind a glass bead as a sign of thanks to nature for the food.

The women also sewed new clothing from deerskins. They used porcupine quills and beads to decorate the shirts and moccasins. They wove bird feathers into cloaks and headdresses for ceremonies.

While the women worked in the fields, the men spent much of their time hunting and fishing. They hunted large animals like deer, bear, and buffalo with bows and arrows. The men used blowguns to shoot small animals like rabbits and squirrels. The guns worked by blowing sharp wood darts through a long piece of hollow cane. They put feathers on the end of the dart to make it fly fast and straight. Men also fished for trout, catfish, and bass in the lakes and rivers. They used nets, traps, and spears. If they caught many fish, the women smoked them over a fire to preserve them.

A Cherokee demonstrates how to use a traditional blowgun.

Artist John White illustrated the Native American way of cooking fish in 1585.

In the winter, men often left the town to hunt. Some hunting trips lasted several months. The men hunted not only for family meals, but also for feasts and ceremonies held throughout the year.

TOWN LIVING

The Cherokee often had to protect their land and towns from neighboring tribes. Early Cherokee towns were surrounded by tall wooden fences, called palisades, to protect them from enemy attacks. The towns looked like forts. Canoes made from hollowed-out trees were kept tied up at nearby waterways. These "dugouts" were large enough to hold up to 20 warriors.

Other than walking, canoes were the Cherokee's only source of transportation.

19

The Cherokee built their houses around a large council house, placed at the center of town. They kept an open plaza clear in front of the council house to use for dances and ceremonies. The council house was used for important meetings. It was large enough for everyone in town to attend.

Meetings were called by the town's elders and two chiefs—the war chief and the peace chief. The chiefs gathered around a sacred fire that was always kept

The council house was also used for weddings.

burning inside the council house. Meetings were more common in times of war when the people needed to discuss war plans. Some women even fought in wars, and gave their opinions about the war plan.

Inside the council house, people sat in sections by clan. A clan is a group of people related by a common ancestor. In every Cherokee town, there were the same seven clans. The town depended on each clan to take care of certain tasks. The Wolf Clan were warriors who protected the people. The Deer Clan were hunters, and

Each clan, represented by symbols at the top of this painting, chose an "honored woman" to be a spokesperson for the clan.

21

the Bird Clan were messengers. The Paint Clan were medicine people, while the Blue Clan were medicine people just for children. The Long Hair Clan kept and taught the town's traditions and history, while the Wild Potato Clan gathered and taught plant knowledge.

Each clan included grandparents, parents, unmarried sisters and brothers, and children who were all related to a female ancestor. When visitors came from another town, they stayed with the people of their clan. Young people had to marry someone from a different clan. When young people married, they lived with the bride's clan.

Clan members took care of the children together. Everything a child learned was taught

A white blanket is wrapped around the couple at a traditional Cherokee wedding.

by his or her mother or one of the mother's family members. Fathers, meanwhile, were responsible for providing food and protection for the family and town.

Mothers, grandmothers, and aunts showed girls how to prepare food, make baskets, and sew clothing. Grandfathers and uncles trained boys to hunt and fish. Uncles taught them about the habits of deer and showed them how to make bows and arrows. They also taught them to play a rough ball game that looked like lacrosse but was much faster. Young men and boys shoved and pushed to get the ball to the goal. Ball games, along with hunting and war, earned Cherokee men respect.

Basket making continues to be an important craft in Cherokee culture.

23

The medicine man or woman was a very important member of a Cherokee town. He or she came to every council meeting, wedding, and ball game. When the men prepared for war or a hunt, the medicine person told them how to get ready.

When the Cherokee became sick, they expected medicine people to heal them. The medicine person studied for years with an older medicine person to learn how to use plants for healing. The medicine person knew, for example, that mint or blackberry plants would help an upset stomach. The Cherokee believed that the Creator gave them these special plants to help them when they got sick.

Medicine people used the roots of cattail plants to prevent illness.

24

IN BALANCE WITH NATURE

Nature was very important to the Cherokee. They believed they could take only what they needed from nature, in order to keep a balance in the world. In Cherokee legends, the people, animals, and plants share the world. If the people do something wrong, such as kill an animal for sport, the balance is disturbed. Then the people might become sick, or the crops might die. Prayers were often said to keep the natural balance safe. For example, after Cherokee men killed a deer, they thanked the animal for the food.

In Cherokee culture, some animals take on certain roles. For example, the owl is the symbol for death.

25

To help keep the balance with nature, the Cherokee also held six traditional ceremonies each year. The time for the ceremonies depended on the moon. The First New Moon of Spring ceremony was a celebration of the new growing season. Other ceremonies marked the first ears of corn in June or July and harvest time 45 days later.

The Great New Moon Festival was an important ceremony that occurred about 10 days after the first moon of fall. This ceremony marked the Cherokee new year and announced a new start for the people. To prepare for the new year, they cleaned their houses and the council house, sent hunters out for deer meat for a feast, and burned old clothing and household goods. The medicine person lit a new fire in the council house. Then each family took a coal to light a fresh fire at home.

A Cherokee artist carves a ceremonial mask.

"WE HAVE NOW GIVEN THE WHITE MEN ENOUGH LAND"

In 1540, Hernando de Soto, a Spanish explorer, led more than 600 men into Cherokee land in present-day South Carolina. De Soto, who had started his trip in present-day Florida, was looking for gold. In their travels, the Spanish explorers often stole food and forced the Indians they met into slavery.

An 1874 Currier and Ives print shows Hernando de Soto and his followers reaching the Mississippi River.

The first Cherokee town the explorers came to was nearly deserted. The people had left because they had heard about the explorers' cruelty from neighboring tribes. But in the next Cherokee town, the people welcomed the explorers and gave them food. After staying overnight, de Soto and his men moved on in their search for gold. These explorers were the first Europeans to write about the Cherokee.

Toward the end of the 1600s, British traders began to cross the mountains from Virginia. They brought guns, metal tools, cloth, and glass beads. The Cherokee traded tanned deer hides, which were popular in Europe. The Europeans used the soft leather to make gloves and book covers.

In 1698, shortly after their first contact with the traders, the Cherokee became sick with smallpox. At least twice during the 1700s, the Cherokee faced smallpox and measles epidemics. They had no way to fight the illnesses, and many of them died.

The medicine people used all of their knowledge, but still their people died. Many Cherokee lost respect for their medicine people and started seeing European doctors. The people felt hopeless and confused because they got sick even though they had kept the balance with nature.

In the 1700s, France, England, and Spain fought for the new land in North America. More settlers moved into Cherokee lands from the east and the north. When the

This Frederic Remington illustration shows a fur trapper and trader in a wooded area.

Cherokee warriors and British soldiers hide from their enemy on their way to warn a nearby fort of a French attack.

French and Indian War (1754–1763) broke out, both England and France tried to make alliances with the different Indian tribes. The Cherokee joined with the British in their fight against the French because their trading ties with the British were tighter.

Although the Cherokee agreed to help the British in the war, many British settlers did not trust the Cherokee. Settlers in Virginia killed more than 20 Cherokee warriors. The Cherokee then began raiding settlements in South Carolina. The governor of South Carolina declared war on the Cherokee. By the end of the French and Indian War, the settlers had pushed the Cherokee off much of their land. Settlers burned Cherokee towns and chased them out of the valleys and into the mountains.

A messenger warns settlers that "the Cherokee are coming."

Before the Cherokee had time to completely recover, the settlers declared war on the British in 1775. Because of their experience with the settlers in South Carolina, the Cherokee allied with the British against the new Americans. After some success in the war, the Americans drove the Cherokee back from their growing cities. They burned more than 50 Cherokee towns, burned their crops, and killed their cattle and horses.

As early as 1768, Chief Oconostota had told the settlers, "We have now given the white men enough land to live on." But by 1800, the Americans had forced the Cherokee to sign away more than half of their land. Every time the Cherokee thought they had made peace, more settlers moved onto their land.

Chief Oconostota

"OUR COUNTRY AND OUR PEOPLE"

By the early 1800s, the Cherokee adopted many American ways. The women readily learned to spin cotton and wool into cloth. Soon, their cloth brought in more money than animal hides. Christian missionaries came to Cherokee towns and set up schools. Many Cherokee became Christians.

For many years, the Cherokee did not have a written language. Instead, storytellers memorized the history and traditions. But in 1821, a Cherokee man named Sequoyah

Sequoyah

33

completed a system to write down the Cherokee language. Both old and young found it easy to learn, and many people quickly learned to read Cherokee.

In 1828, another Cherokee, Elias Boudinot, began to print a newspaper written in both Cherokee and English.

The Cherokee Phoenix *printed articles in English and Cherokee.*

The Cherokee Phoenix began printing articles from the Cherokee point of view. Some of these articles were printed in English newspapers all over the United States.

In less than 30 years, the Cherokee adopted the American way of life. Their leaders admired the U.S. Constitution. In 1827, they wrote a new constitution for the Cherokee nation.

They built a capital at New Echota, Georgia, with a council house, a court building, and an office for *The Cherokee Phoenix*. The people elected John Ross as their first chief. Ross was known for his leadership, and both Cherokee and white people respected him.

But the American population was growing in nearby states. Settlers wanted more land for farms. In 1830, the U.S. government passed a law that forced all Indians in the eastern states to move west of the Mississippi River. This new land, in what is now the state of Oklahoma, was called Indian Territory.

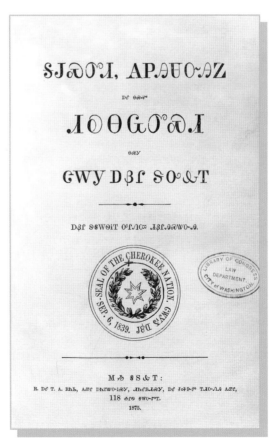

The cover of a printed version of the constitution and laws of the Cherokee nation.

Major Ridge was one of the leaders who signed the treaty that gave up Cherokee homelands.

The Cherokee were divided about moving west. Most did not want to leave their homeland, but some thought it might be the only way to avoid more fighting. In 1835, feeling they had no choice, some Cherokee leaders signed a treaty agreeing to move west. They believed the Cherokee people would face more difficulties from the Americans if they tried to stay.

Knowing that most of his people wanted to stay, Chief Ross did not sign the treaty. But the Cherokee were forced to leave their homeland anyway. The government ignored earlier treaties and sent soldiers to take the Cherokee to Indian Territory in the Trail of Tears journey.

When the last Cherokee arrived in Indian Territory in 1839, the people worked to start new lives for themselves. They began to set up homes, schools, and churches. Chief Ross called a council meeting, and in September 1839, he was elected chief once again. The leaders wrote a new constitution and decided that one of their new towns, Tahlequah, would be their new capital. In 1846, the U.S. government recognized the Western Cherokee as the owners of the Indian Territory land.

As Chief Ross wrote in 1834, "Our country and our people should always be our motto." Thousands of Cherokee had died, and the survivors were forced to leave their homelands and way of life. Yet, the Cherokee people lived on.

John Ross

THE CHEROKEE TODAY

Many times in the past, the Cherokee feared they might disappear. But today, the people continue to grow and change. Wilma Mankiller, a former Cherokee chief, has said, "Not only do we exist, but we're thriving and we're growing, and we're learning now to trust our own thinking again and dig our way out."

Wilma Mankiller was the first Cherokee woman elected as chief.

The United States recognizes three Cherokee tribes. The Cherokee Nation of Oklahoma is the largest. The tribal government runs an electronics factory, several casinos, and a golf course. The government has improved housing, built medical clinics, and improved tribal schools. *The Cherokee Phoenix* is still published monthly in English and Cherokee.

A second tribe, the United Keetoowah Band, is also in Oklahoma. The tribe runs a bingo hall and provides services like housing and child care to its members.

The third band, the Eastern Band of Cherokee, has land in western North Carolina. This band escaped from the soldiers in 1839. Today, the Eastern Cherokee have a traditional village, a play about Cherokee history, and craft shops. They sell traditional baskets, pots, and carvings to tourists every summer.

The Cherokee language is still spoken by thousands of Cherokee. It is taught in schools and used in church services. The Cherokee Nation of Oklahoma has developed

Although not federally recognized, the Echota Cherokee Tribe is recognized by the state of Alabama. Pictured is a tribal singing group, the Cherokee Road Singers.

online courses to teach the Cherokee language. As Chief Chad Smith says, "Our language is one of the things that make Cherokee people special. We owe it to our children to teach them Cherokee, to pass on that part of our legacy. It is the foundation of our culture."

While preserving their language and history, the Cherokee look forward to the future. Their leaders work to make sure the people have all they need to live in today's world. Strong leadership and the ability to adjust to change have helped the Cherokee become a vibrant, modern nation.

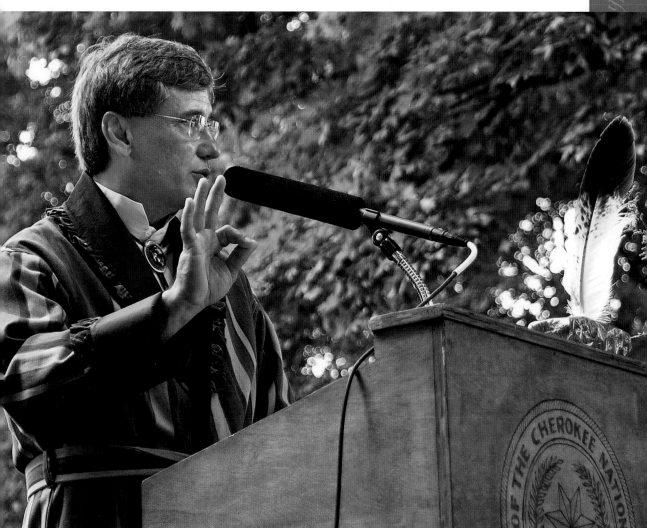

Chief Chad Smith delivers a speech during a Cherokee celebration in September 2004.

GLOSSARY

alliances—agreements between nations or groups of people to work together

ceremony—traditional prayer or dance used to celebrate a special occasion

clan—a group of people related by a common ancestor

epidemics—severe outbreaks of an infectious disease

lacrosse—a game that is played using sticks with a net on one end to throw, catch, and carry a ball to a goal

medicine people—men and women who used certain plants to cure illness

palisades—tall fences built around a Cherokee village to keep enemies out

plaza—public square or open space often used for ceremonies

reservations—large areas of land set aside for Native Americans; in Canada, reservations are called reserves

treaty—a formal agreement between groups or nations

DID YOU KNOW?

- Original Cherokee lands covered parts of present-day West Virginia, Virginia, North Carolina, South Carolina, Kentucky, Tennessee, Georgia, and Alabama.

- Tennessee takes its name from a Cherokee town called Tanasi.

- In the Stomp Dance, a traditional Cherokee dance, women dancers tied turtle shells filled with pebbles to their legs. These rattles kept the beat when they danced. Today, they often use empty tin cans instead of shells.

- In a traditional Cherokee wedding, the woman gives the man an ear of corn to show that she will care for the household. The man gives the woman deer meat to show he will provide for the family.

- Today, most Cherokee Indians have both an English name and a Cherokee name. The grandmother on the mother's side often gives her grandchildren their Cherokee names.

IMPORTANT DATES

Timeline

1540	Hernando de Soto meets the Cherokee in the southeastern United States.
1754	The French and Indian War is fought.
1775	The Cherokee fight the Americans in the Revolutionary War.
1821	Sequoyah creates a Cherokee system of writing.
1827	Cherokee write their first constitution.
1830	Indian Removal Act forces Indians to leave their homeland and move west.
1835	Some Cherokee leaders sign the Treaty of New Echota and agree to move west.
1838	The U.S. government forces the Cherokee to move to Indian Territory (Oklahoma); many die on the Trail of Tears.
1839	The Cherokee write a new constitution.
1846	The U.S. government recognizes Western Cherokee as owners of their land in Indian Territory.
1987	Wilma Mankiller is elected the first woman principal chief of the Cherokee Nation.

IMPORTANT PEOPLE

ELIAS BOUDINOT (1804?–1839)
Started first Cherokee newspaper, The Cherokee Phoenix, *in 1828*

WILMA MANKILLER (1945–)
First Cherokee woman elected as chief; she was appointed in 1985, officially elected in 1987, and served until 1995

JOHN ROSS (1790–1860)
Elected first Cherokee chief in 1828 and guided his people through the move to Indian Territory (Oklahoma)

SEQUOYAH (1770?–1843)
Cherokee who created a system to write the Cherokee language; the giant sequoia tree is named after him

WANT TO KNOW MORE?

At the Library

Dennis, Yvonne Wakim. *Sequoyah: 1770?-1843*. Mankato, Minn.: Blue
Earth Books, 2004.

Duvall, Deborah. *How Rabbit Lost His Tail: A Traditional Cherokee Legend*.
Albuquerque: University of New Mexico Press, 2003.

Furbee, Mary. *Wild Rose: Nancy Ward and the Cherokee Nation.* Greensboro,
N.C.: Morgan Reynolds Publishing, 2001.

Sonneborn, Liz. *The Cherokee.* New York: Franklin Watts, 2003.

On the Web

For more information on this topic, use FactHound.

1. Go to *www.facthound.com*

2. Type in this book ID: 0756512735

3. Click on the *Fetch It* button.

FactHound will find the best Web sites for you.

On the Road

Cherokee Heritage Center
21192 S. Keeler Drive
Park Hill, OK 74451
918/456-6007
To see an ancient village that shows Cherokee basket weavers, potters, and the traditional Cherokee game of stickball

Trail of Tears State Park
429 Moccasin Springs
Jackson, MO 63755
573/334-1711
To see two miles (three kilometers) of the original Trail of Tears and a visitor center that offers programs on Cherokee cultural history

Look for more We the People books about this era:

The Alamo
The Arapaho and Their History
The Battle of the Little Bighorn
The Buffalo Soldiers
The California Gold Rush
The Chumash and Their History
The Creek and Their History
The Erie Canal
Great Women of Pioneer America
Great Women of the Old West
The Iroquois and Their History
The Lewis and Clark Expedition
The Louisiana Purchase

The Mexican War
The Ojibwe and Their History
The Oregon Trail
The Pony Express
The Powhatan and Their History
The Pueblo and Their History
The Santa Fe Trail
The Sioux and Their History
The Trail of Tears
The Transcontinental Railroad
The Wampanoag and Their History
The War of 1812

A complete list of We the People titles is available on our Web site:
www.compasspointbooks.com

47

INDEX

Appalachian Mountains, 4, 8, 9, 12, 14

ball games, 23, 24
Bird Clan, 22
blowguns, 17
Blue Clan, 22
Boudinot, Elias, 34

canoes, 19
ceremonies, 16, 18, 20 26
The Cherokee Phoenix newspaper, 34, 35, 39
Cherokee Nation of Oklahoma, 13, 39–40
chiefs, 5, 20–21, 35, 37, 38
children, 8, 16, 22–23
clans, 21–22
clothing, 9, 10, 16, 23, 26
constitution, 34, 37
corn, 15, 16
council house, 20, 21, 26, 35
council meetings, 20–21, 24, 37
Creek Indians, 10

Deer Clan, 21
diseases, 6, 8, 28
dugout canoes, 19

Eastern Band of Cherokee, 39
farming, 10, 15–16, 26
First New Moon of Spring

ceremony, 26
fishing, 17, 23
food, 9, 15, 16, 18, 23, 25, 27, 28
French and Indian War, 30–31
fur trade, 10, 28

gathering, 16
gold, 27, 28
Great New Moon Festival, 26

houses, 10, 14–15, 16, 20, 26
hunting, 17, 18, 23, 24, 25, 26

Indian Removal Act, 10–11
Indian Territory, 4, 7, 11, 35, 36–37

Jackson, Andrew, 12

language, 10, 33–34, 39, 40
Long Hair Clan, 22

Mankiller, Wilma (chief), 38
marriage, 22, 24
medicine people, 22, 24, 26, 29
men, 8, 17, 18, 23, 24, 25
missionaries, 33

name, 10

Oconostota (chief), 32

Paint Clan, 22

palisades, 19
peace chiefs, 20
population, 12

religion, 25–26, 33
reservations, 12
Ross, John (chief), 5, 6, 8, 35, 36, 37

sacred fire, 20–21, 26
Scott, Winfield, 4
Sequoyah, 33–34
settlers, 29, 31, 32, 35
slavery, 27
smallpox, 28
Smith, Chad (chief), 40
Soto, Hernando de, 27, 28
Spanish exploration, 27–28
Supreme Court, 11–12

towns, 10, 14, 16, 19, 20, 21, 22, 23, 24, 28, 31, 32, 33, 37
Trail of Tears, 8, 36
Trail Where They Cried, 8
treaties, 36

United Keetoowah Band, 39

war chiefs, 20
Wild Potato Clan, 22
Wolf Clan, 21
women, 8, 10, 16, 17, 21, 22, 23, 33

About the Author

Mary Englar is a freelance writer and a teacher of English and creative writing. She has a Master of Fine Arts degree in writing from Minnesota State University, Mankato, and has written more than 30 nonfiction books for children. She continues to read and write about the many different cultures of our world from her home in Minnesota.